Fishing in the North Woods

Fishing
IN THE NORTH WOODS

WINSLOW HOMER

David Tatham
Foreword by Tom Rosenbauer
Guideboat section by Hallie E. Bond

MUSEUM OF FINE ARTS, BOSTON
in association with
UNIVERSE PUBLISHING

Frontispiece: Winslow Homer, "Fly Fishing, Saranac Lake," 1889

Except where otherwise indicated, all works of art in this
volume are by Winslow Homer.

The publishers wish to thank the National Gallery of Art for
granting permission to reprint "Winslow Homer at the North
Woods Club" by David Tatham. This article originally appeared
in slightly different form in *Winslow Homer, A Symposium*, copyright
© 1990 Trustees of the National Gallery of Art, Washington.

Permission to use material from *The North Woods Club 1886–1986,*
copyright © 1986 by Leila Fosburgh Wilson, is gratefully acknowl-
edged.

First published in the United States of America in 1995
by UNIVERSE PUBLISHING
A Division of Rizzoli International Publications, Inc.
300 Park Avenue South
New York, NY 10010

95 96 97 98 99 / 10 9 8 7 6 5 4 3 2 1

Library of Congress catalog card number 95–060811
ISBN: 0-7893-0016-8

Design and typography by Russell Hassell
Printed in Singapore

Contents

"The Rise," 1900

Foreword

by Tom Rosenbauer

Winslow Homer's watercolors of fishing scenes have the power to delight and inspire those who have never held a rod in their hands. Looking at these paintings, though, the fly-fisher is transported to a time before outboard motors and acid rain, when a quiet morning on an Adirondack lake might yield wild trout dinners for an entire camp. This was a painter who knew how to play a wildly leaping salmon, could curve a silk line through the air, and knew when the right fly might be a Red Ibis instead of a Black Gnat. A fisherman all his life, Homer arranged long fishing (and painting) trips to the Adirondack lakes and to the wilder waters of Quebec during the last forty years of his life, from the 1870s to just before his death in 1910. Anglers today can well envy the month-long trips and less heavily fished waters available to sportsmen of Homer's days.

Much of Winslow Homer's fishing occurred at a simple Adirondack camp, where sportsmen of his day could enjoy creature comforts in the evening yet still spend a day on a wilderness lake.

What was a day on the water like then? The only sounds to compete with the wail of a loon on those mornings must have been the creak of oars on a wooden boat and the distant thunk of someone cutting wood for the cooking fires. Stare at "The Rise" for a few moments and you'll start to hear those sounds.

Homer probably used wet, or sunken, flies exclusively. After hundreds of years of catching trout with flies beneath the surface of the water, fishermen in the Victorian era were just starting to experiment with flies that floated, but these were used on the more sophisticated brown trout of the Catskills and Pennsylvania streams. The

"Jumping Trout," 1889

Fly wallet with drawings and tied flies, 1883

"A Fisherman's Day," 1889

more easily fooled brook trout, the native trout of the Adirondacks, depicted in watercolors like "Jumping Trout," were perfectly content to strike a gaudy Red Ibis. Fishermen of Homer's day typically used a minimum of three flies at once on a leader, and sometimes up to twelve at one time. The flies would have been snelled, or already attached to loops, so they could be easily fastened to the leader.

Unlike earlier in the century, when most flies were English patterns borrowed for use on our waters, Homer likely also used such indigenous American patterns as the Parmachene Belle or the Montreal. By 1892, Mary Orvis Marbury had catalogued two hundred and ninety fly patterns in her book *Favorite Flies and Their Histories*, most of them gaudy American patterns. This was the Victorian era, and fly dressers had at their disposal the excesses of the millinery trade, with exotic feathers from around the world such as ibis, peacock, toucan, macaw, jungle cock, and bustard. By the time Homer died, the newly formed Audubon Society had encouraged legislation that made trade in most of these feathers illegal and today fly tiers get by with substitutes.

Victorian anglers like Homer were walking geography lessons, and not just because of flies with exotic feathers. Although the best rods were made in the United States, the bamboo used to make them came from China. The finest fly reels were made in England, however American reel makers such as Orvis and Meisselbach were giving the English a run for their money. Silkworm gut leaders came from

Top to bottom: contemporary Parmachene Belle, Red Ibis, and Montreal flies

England, China, or Spain. Silk fly lines came from England, France, or Spain.

Winslow Homer's rod and case

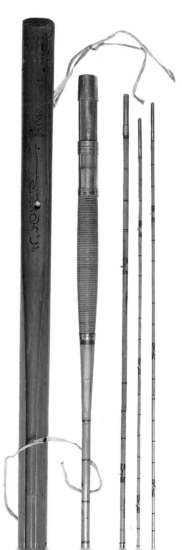

Prior to the 1870s, most fly rods were long and as limber as a green willow branch. They would be up to eighteen feet in length for a salmon rod down to about twelve feet long for a trout rod. They might weigh anywhere from almost a pound for the big salmon rods down to four ounces for a "ladies rod." These early rods were made from any number of native or exotic woods: hickory, juniper, lancewood, greenheart, yew, and ash being just a few of the woods that were used. Then, a revolution took place. Rod makers began to cut tapered strips from Asian bamboo and glue them together. This produced a rod that was stronger, stiffer, and more powerful than any rod ever made. Six strips were most common, though rods made with four and even twelve strips of bamboo were tried. The one authenticated rod of Homer's, in the collection of The American Museum of Fly Fishing, is a nine-and-a-half-foot rod of six-strip split bamboo.

In many of Homer's watercolors that depict fishing for land-locked salmon (more popularly known in Homer's day by its Quebecois name, ouananiche), a five-pound salmon which decided to go in the opposite direction from the canoe in heavy water could

"Under The Falls, the Grand Discharge," 1895

not have been landed with the soft fly rods made in the 1860s. So we can assume that Homer's tackle was state-of-the-art for his time.

After a day on the water, Homer (or his guide) would have to carefully remove all the braided and oiled silk fly line from his reel and store it on a line winder, as these organic lines were prone to rot and mildew. Flies he had used that day would be left to dry before being returned to his sheepskin fly book so the hooks would not rust. And as we know Homer was fastidious about his dress, we can assume that he would take great care to dry off his rod before replacing it in its case, since the split bamboo was joined with animal glues that

Line winder and reel

are not waterproof and, despite the five coats of varnish applied to protect them from the elements, too much moisture could ruin a prized possession.

The biggest difference between watching Homer in a boat on an Adirondack lake and watching a modern fly fisher would be the intensity of the motions. Whereas most fly fishers of the 1990s would be trying to cast seventy-five feet of line and rowing at full speed to every rise, fly-fishing in Homer's time was less intent on goals, more on the essence of fly-fishing that came easier to a nineteenth-century romantic than to most of us today. Look at "Two Men in a Canoe":

the fisherman with his elbow poised just above his waist, moving only his forearm and wrist, not rocking the boat a bit with his casting stroke. Unhurried. We should be thankful to Homer for showing us nature, man, and fly-fishing in a way far superior to either the photographs or the writing of his day.

"Two Men in a Canoe," 1895

The Lure of the North Woods

FEW FULLY UNDERSTAND *what the Adirondack wilderness really is. It is a mystery even to those who have crossed and recrossed it by boats along its avenues—the lakes; and on foot through its vast and silent recesses.... Though the woodman may pass his lifetime in some section of the wilderness, it is still a mystery to him.* —VERPLANCK COLVIN, 1879

Opposite: "Adirondack Lake" (detail), 1889

In 1869, a little book called *Adventures in the Wilderness; or, Camp-Life in the Adirondacks* caught the imagination of the public. It was an enthusiastic guide to the Adirondack wilderness area of New York State and was written by William H. H. Murray, who was at that time the minister of the prestigious Park Street Church in Boston. In it, Murray not only told wonderful anecdotes of the native guides, the plentiful fish, and the healthful mountain air, he also told exactly how to make travel plans, what to bring, and how much it would cost. The book went into multiple printings and encouraged so many adventure seekers to travel to the north woods that William Murray quickly became known as Adirondack Murray. Some of Murray's readers reported that he exaggerated the abundance of fish, game, and guides and sadly underestimated the nuisance of fiercely biting blackflies.

"Adirondack Lake," 1889

"Old Settlers,"
1892

"Fishing in the Adirondacks"

"Leaping Trout," 1889

READER, DID YOU EVER LAND A TROUT? *I do not ask if you ever jerked some poor little fellow out of a brook three feet across, with a pole six inches around at the butt, and so heavy as to require both hands and feet well braced to hold it out. No, that's not landing a trout. But did you ever sit in a boat, with nine ounces of lance-wood for a rod, and two hundred feet of braided silk in your double-acting reel, and hook a trout whose strain brought tip and butt together as you checked him in some wild flight, and tested your quivering line from gut to reel-knot?* —ADIRONDACK MURRAY

WHAT A TRIP *you will have had, what wonders seen, what rare experiences enjoyed! How many evenings will pass on golden wings at home, as friends draw close their circle around the glowing grate and listen as you rehearse the story of your adventures—shoot over again your "first buck" and land for the hundredth time your "biggest" trout!*
—ADIRONDACK MURRAY

"October Day," 1889

Around the Campfire

WE CUT YOUNG TREES *to make our poles and thwarts,*
Barked the white spruce to weatherfend the roof,
Then struck a light and kindled the camp-fire.
—RALPH WALDO EMERSON

Opposite: "The Adirondack Guide" (detail), 1894

Though Winslow Homer lived at the edge of the sea on Maine's rockbound coast for more than a quarter of a century and became America's great painter of marine subjects, he maintained a longer and equally productive association with inland waters—the lakes and streams in which he fished from youth to old age. Born in Boston in 1836, he moved with his family to Cambridge in 1842 and before the age of twenty became a serious enough angler to rise before dawn and hike to Fresh Pond to fish before the workday began. Throughout the 1860s, when his studio was in New York City, he fished (and painted) during his summer travels in Massachusetts, New Hampshire, New Jersey, and New York. The illustrations he drew for popular magazines in these years showed the sport to be stylish for women and men alike. In 1870, encouraged not only by Adirondack Murray's

"Waiting for a Bite," 1874

enthusiastic descriptions of the scenic beauty, robust life, and bountiful fishing in the mountain wilderness of northern New York, but also by firsthand reports from artist friends who had preceded him there—including John Lee Fitch, Homer Martin, Frederick Rondel, Roswell Shurtleff, and Eliphalet Terry—Homer set out for the Adirondacks with rod and reel as well as paints and brushes. He began a relationship with the region that ended only with his death in 1910. From these Adirondack visits, and his excursions to even

"Ausable River," 1874, photograph by J. F. Murphy. Winslow Homer, with hat and pipe, is in the center of the photograph. Roswell Shurtleff is at the lower right.

wilder sites in Quebec, came a body of work about life in the woods, and especially about fishing, that in originality of concept and execution remains one of the great achievements of American art.

A photograph taken at Keene Valley in 1874 shows Homer with a group of fellow guests from the Widow Beede's Cottage disporting themselves on a nearby rock. Among them is Shurtleff, whose friendship with Homer dated from their days as graphic artists in Boston in the late 1850s. The difference between Shurtleff's dress and Homer's, the former rough and latter dapper, is instructive. By the time of Homer's first sojourn in 1870 the Adirondacks had ample though widely scattered summer hotels and inns, making it possible for tourists to spend a week or a month in stylish comfort. When Shurtleff first visited the region in the 1850s, the lodgings available were few and rudimentary, and he continued to prefer such primitive accommodations throughout his long association with Keene Valley. He had, after all, first been drawn to the Adirondacks by its reputation as the least explored mountain wilderness in the eastern United States and had been part of the first wave of artists to develop a sustained interest in the area.

The one subject in American painting that is distinctive to the
Adirondacks—scenes of camp life—was invented by these artists in
the 1850s. The two essential components of the subject are a group
of sportsmen ("sports") relaxing in a forest clearing, often accompanied by one or more guides, and a lean-to shanty or tent. No
women are present, or even within miles, presumably. The sports are
outsiders to the forest, attended by insiders, the guides; they are men
from town dependent on the man of the woods. Freed from the
cares of home, job, and society, and with the satisfactions of a day of
hunting or fishing behind them, they take their ease. The camp
scene subjects of the 1850s pictorially document the shift then
underway in American thought in which a pantheistic concept of
the natural world as the Almighty's hallowed residence surrendered

Copper candleholder

its primacy to the more prosaic notion of nature as everyone's playground. The natural world of the camp scenes of the 1850s ministers to the body at least as much as to the spirit.

Perhaps the best known example of the camp scene genre is William J. Stillman's "Philosopher's Camp." It records and idealizes the pilgrimage to wilderness of ten distinguished men from Cambridge and Boston—Ralph Waldo Emerson, James Russell Lowell, and Louis Agassiz among them—men whose natural environment was the study, library, laboratory, and lecture hall. Like Henry David Thoreau (who had declined to join the group) at Walden Pond, these philosophers sought to learn what nature at its purest had to teach. Stillman made the arrangements, providing one guide and one guideboat for each man in the party. Leaving from Martin's

William J. Stillman, "The Philosopher's Camp in the Adirondacks," 1858

Frederic Rondel, "A Hunting Party in the Woods," 1856

Creel

Hotel on Saranac Lake, the guides rowed and "carried" (portaged) the group and their gear to Follansby Pond. Near water's edge the guides built camp, cooked the trout caught by these distinguished visitors, and aided them in their hunt for deer. Though Stillman took little notice of the guides in his painting, they were essential to the success of any camping expedition in the wilderness.

One of the most animated and endearing products of the camp scene genre is Frederic Rondel's "A Hunting Party in the Woods" of 1856. These sportsmen play cards, clean weapons, count fish, smoke, dine, and drink. Through a series of not very subtle pictorial cues, Rondel leads the eye across the canvas, figure by figure, from the yawning lean-to, to the table at the right spread sparsely with food and wine. Propped open against a forward pole of the lean-to is a paint box with an oil sketch of a mountain landscape in its lid and a prepared palette and brushes resting on top. It is set between a gun and an ax for the amusement of future iconographers. The paint box presumably belongs to Rondel, who is shown with a pipe in his hand seated on a stump.

Homer's major contribution to the camp scene genre came in 1880 with his oil "Camp Fire." Stripped of the anecdotal detail found in examples of the 1850s, it stands alone as the culmination of the type, making all earlier treatments of the subject seem contrived and awkward. The somnolent atmosphere is an appropriate expression of the essential idea of relaxation after a day of hunting or fishing. A wickerwork creel rests on the outer edge of the lean-to's bough covered platform, and an angler's net hangs against one of its poles. Out of sight are the long, sectioned, bamboo fishing poles whose introduction to the United States in the 1840s began the sequence of advances in fishing tackle design that by 1880 had greatly increased and refined the sportman's chances for success. The rendering of the fire and the sparks that fly from it has been admired for its naturalism since the painting's first exhibition. This canvas seems to have exhausted Homer's interest in camp scenes, however, for his later Adirondack works treat the active life of the woods, the men of the woods, and the woods alone. Indeed by 1880 the older genre was passing from popularity, to be revived briefly in the 1890s in both painting and illustration by Frederic Remington.

Long-handled collapsible landing net

Homer's "Camp Fire" shares with his Gloucester harbor watercolors of 1880 a keen and exploratory interest in unusual conditions of light. Light is as much the painting's subject as is camp life. Homer may have adapted some of the composition of "Camp Fire" from his Adirondack drawings of 1874, very possibly those that had served as the basis for his "Camping Out in the Adirondack Mountains," which was published as a wood engraving by *Harper's Weekly* in 1874.

"Camp Fire," 1880

THE PAINTING *"was so real, a woodsman could tell what kind of logs were burning by the sparks that rose in long curved lines."*
—ROSWELL M. SHURTLEFF

Homer at the North Woods Club

I HAVE BEEN HERE MYSELF JUST A WEEK. *The virgin forest comes close to our house, and the diversity of walks through it, the brooks and the ascensions of hilltops are infinite. I doubt if there be anything like it in Europe. Your mountains are grander, but you have nowhere this carpet of absolutely primitive forest, with its indescribably sweet exhalations, spreading in every direction unbroken. I shall stay here doing hardly any work till late in September. I need to lead a purely animal life for at least two months to carry me through the teaching year.* —WILLIAM JAMES, *writing from Keene Valley, 1883*

Opposite: "Hudson River" (detail), 1892

The eminent philosopher William James wrote these words in Keene Valley, where Winslow Homer had fished and painted nearly a decade earlier. James wrote from the Putnam Camp, one of many private clubs established in the Adirondacks in the 1880s to preserve for outdoor recreation tracts of forestland endangered by the arrival of large-scale logging operations. About thirty miles to the southwest as the crow flies, in the township of Minerva, an association later known as the North Woods Club came into being at a site where Homer had fished and painted in the 1870s. The club offered a forest experience that was a far cry from the camp life portrayed in the paintings of the 1850s. Perhaps the most striking difference was the presence of women, most of whom were wives, sisters, mothers, daughters, and friends of members.

Eliphalet Terry, "Log Cabin Near North Woods Club," ca. 1857

Homer had first visited this site in 1870, probably on the advice of the painter Eliphalet Terry, a fellow member of the Century Club in New York City and an avid fisherman. Homer stayed in a log farmhouse built by the Reverend Thomas Baker, a disillusioned abolitionist who, with his wife Eunice and daughter Juliette, had gone in the mid-1850s to this remote forest clearing and with unremitting hard labor had made a farm of it. They

soon began to accommodate summer boarders from New York and elsewhere, some of whom came to fish in the seven large ponds located on the Baker's land, within a mile or two of the farmhouse. After Thomas Baker's death in 1862, his widow and their daughter ran the farm with the help of hired hands. Terry had been a summer boarder since 1859. When Eunice and Juliette, and a younger daughter, Jennie, spent winter months with relatives near New York, he entertained them, and this may have been how Homer met these remarkably resourceful women who presided over a tract of five thousand acres.

Over a span of four decades, Homer spent a total of at least seventy-six weeks there. From these visits came a number of drawings, five wood engravings, a dozen oils, and about a hundred watercolors. There is never any satisfactory accounting for the impact of place on an artist, but in Homer's case we can comprehend well enough the mix of visual, social, and sporting ingredients that, compounded early at Baker's clearing, proved to be a powerful and durable attraction for him.

When Homer returned to the Adirondacks in 1889, Baker's clearing was no longer a farm but the meadow-like campus of a private

"Hudson River," 1892

THE BAKERS *(and a few hired men) lumbered in winter, farmed the cleared*
land in summer, and took on boarders.... The workload was fantastic and includ-
ed the clearing of woodlands, preparing of timber for commercial sale, the cutting
of firewood, and the making of every necessity such as furnishings, shingles, and
sap buckets for spring sugaring.... —LEILA FOSBURGH WILSON

club. It had been purchased in 1887 by a group of New Yorkers who had incorporated themselves the previous year as The Adirondack Preserve Association for the Encouragement of Social Pastimes and the Preservation of Game and Forests. Confusion of this name with those of other organizations, and even with the newly formed state

park, led to a change in 1895 to the North Woods Club. By this time, the club's property consisted of some five thousand acres of mountainous forest, ponds, and streams surrounding the clearing.

"North Woods Club," 1895, photograph by Verplanck Colvin

Charles Savage Homer, Jr., two years older than his brother Winslow, was also an expert fisherman. The two have often been described as charter members of the North Woods Club, but they were not. Homer was elected to membership on 28 January 1888 in the club's second year and a month before his fifty-second birthday. He made his return to the Baker's log house under its new ownership the following year. Homer's first visits to the club were lengthy—a total of eighteen weeks in 1889, seven weeks in 1891, and nine weeks in 1892—divided into early and late season stays, probably to allow him to spend the height of the summer at Prout's Neck and to avoid the worst of the blackfly season in the

"An Unexpected Catch," 1890

THE ORIGINAL OBJECTIVES *of the Club are duly recorded: "boating, fishing, athletic and all manly, lawful sports and pastimes, and the preservation of game and forests."*
—LEILA FOSBURGH WILSON

Adirondacks. His later visits ranged from one to five weeks, usually in
May and June.

The main lodge at the North Woods Club was rustic, but it
offered far more amenities than a tent or lean-to. A dining hall was
located next door. By the 1890s some members, Terry among them,
had built their own cottages, while still dining communally. Terry's
cottage, a stone's throw from the clubhouse (as the Baker's log house
was now known), was a small building having little in common with
the baronial lodges then rising elsewhere in the Adirondacks, but it
accommodated a few people. Homer often bunked there, even after
Terry's death in 1895. Only occasionally did their visits coincide.
Members came mostly from New York City and its environs, but also

IT WAS HERE *(at the North Woods Club) that Winslow Homer painted and sketched almost all his Adirondack pictures.* —LEILA FOSBURGH WILSON

"Pickerel Fishing," 1892

with strong contingents from Pittsburgh and Wilmington. In the mid-1890s through at least 1906 the annual dues were fifty dollars. In the mid-1890s board was $1.75 a day.

Guides were available at twenty-five cents an hour or $2.50 a day, $3.00 with a dog. This rate was probably equivalent to what Homer paid those who modeled for him.

Homer painted most of his Adirondack watercolors within several hundred yards of the clubhouse, nearly all at locations much frequented by club members then and for more than a century afterward. He painted nothing of the club's social life but a good deal of its sporting life. Guides, sport fisherman, fish, deer, dogs, logging—

"Woodsman and Fallen Tree," 1891

"Mink Pond," 1891

IN 1890 AND 1891 *the New York State Fish Commission provided 100,000 brook-trout fry for stocking Huntley, Beaver, Mink, and Frank, and then, in 1892, provided 20,000 brown-trout fry and 5,000 land-locked salmon plus some black bass for Beaver Pond. In 1906... Thumb was designated for fly fishing only, and by 1911, with a restocking of small-mouth bass, Split Rock was designated for bass only.* —LEILA FOSBURGH WILSON

these subjects recur year after year in Homer's North Woods Club work. Indeed they are all present in the work of his first season at the club. That year, 1889, in the course of eighteen weeks, he produced twenty-five to thirty finished sheets representing a newfound maturity in the medium of watercolor. The bold and steady advances in technique he had made throughout the 1880s culminated here. The radical freedom in color and brushwork of his Gloucester watercolors of 1880, the strong draftsmanship and greater complexity of composition of the watercolors he painted in the English fishing village of Cullercoats during his residence there from 1881 to 1882, and the brilliance of light on water and foliage that gradually emerged in his Caribbean work beginning in 1885—all converged in 1889 and, with the club as a catalyst, burst forth in this extraordinary body of Adirondack watercolors. This was a kind of *annus mirabilis* for Homer as a watercolorist.

"Two Trout," 1889

From the club's lodge, Homer looked out on Beaver Mountain, with its graceful asymmetrical rise. A dark, coniferous ridge contrasted with the lighter, deciduous cover of the rest of the mountain. He included this mountain in more than two dozen works between 1870 and 1902, constantly varying its appearance as he viewed it from different locations. He first depicted it in the background of a wood engraving, "Trapping in the Adirondacks," published in *Every Saturday* in 1870, and included it in "Camping Out in the Adirondack Mountains," published in *Harper's Weekly* in 1874. It forms the background of his well-known "Two Guides," 1875, even though the figures are from

NO MORE THAN TWENTY *trout were to be killed by any one person in a day, and no more than three deer a season. All fish caught were turned in to the kitchen staff for use at the Club table. None could be kept for private consumption or sale.*

—LEILA FOSBURGH WILSON

"Leaping Trout," 1889

"Two Guides," 1875

Keene Valley. It seems likely that the pictorial strengths of the landform, varied by season, hour, and weather, reintroduced themselves to him virtually daily when he was in the Adirondacks and that he responded to what he saw with his usual reportorial verve.

In his depictions of the club's guides Homer pictorially reinforced the concept that they were a part of the natural environment, quite literally men of the woods. These men were widely respected for their skills and character and Homer held them in high regard, just as he had earlier admired the fisherfolk of Cullercoats and the deep-sea fishermen of Maine. He did not portray the guides in a deferential relationship to sportsmen, as had the camp scene painters of the 1850s, nor did he sentimentalize or caricature them, as did many popular illustrators of the day. Rather, he invested them with a dignity that was grounded in Jeffersonian and Jacksonian democratic ideals as well as in his own personal esteem for them.

The figures in Homer's Adirondack watercolors—fly-fishermen, loggers, and guides—who often carry rods, nets, axes, oars, and pikes, live by their hands and by a profound, highly specialized, and not easily verbalized knowledge of complex tasks. Homer's admiration for others' mastery of manual skills seems implicit in his use of his own mastery in portraying them.

The Guide and the Guideboat

NOW, IN THE NORTH WOODS, *owing to their marvellous water-communication, you do all your sporting from your boat. If you wish to go one or ten miles for a "fish," your guide paddles you to the spot, and serves you while you handle the rod. This takes from recreation every trace of toil. You have all the excitement of sporting, without any attending physical weariness.*

—ADIRONDACK MURRAY

Opposite: "The Blue Boat" (detail), 1892

The boat that made sporting so easy for tourists in Murray's day was a light, fast rowing boat, which had evolved in the previous four decades to serve the needs of Adirondack settlers. During the "rush to the wilderness" touched off by Murray's book, many of those settlers supplemented the incomes from their small farms by becoming professional hunting and fishing guides. Their boats were indispensable in guiding, and soon became known as the Adirondack guideboat. Winslow Homer's artistic eye was caught by the character of the Adirondack guides and the functional beauty of their boats, and he painted them often on his trips to the North Woods.

The Adirondack guideboat was ideally suited to the North Woods, a region of many waterways that are frequently narrow, shallow, and broken up by rapids and waterfalls. Murray's "marvellous water-communication" is formed by several major river systems separated only by low divides. A boat for the Adirondacks had to be light enough to be carried around obstructions and from waterway to waterway. For the settlers and later for the sports who spent a month or two roaming the woods in search of deer and trout, it also had to be capacious, to carry all the gear needed for a trip in the days before aluminum campware, and easygoing, to make the work as light as possible for the guide.

These qualities, light weight, speed, and capacity, do not often go together in a wooden boat. The Adirondack guideboat was

"Waterfall in the Adirondacks"

developed largely in isolation by men who were not professionally trained boat builders. It is a tribute to their ingenuity and skill that they developed a boat which even today is regarded as one of the finest types of regional watercraft in the world.

The graceful craft in Homer's "Blue Boat" is clearly an Adirondack guideboat. It can be identified by its shape: the deep but gradual sheer, or sweep, of the gunwales downward from either end to the center, and the fine ends rapidly flaring outward toward the middle of the boat. The two men in it, probably both guides, possibly looking for a good trout hole under an overhanging bank, are maneuvering the boat up one of the narrow, winding streams so common in the Adirondacks. The forward man twists around to help navigate; he was probably rowing out on the lake but has now shipped the oars in the boat. The man in the stern propels the craft with a paddle, standard guideboat equipment for just such occasions as this. Guideboat paddles have long narrow blades, longer than the blades on most canoe paddles, and can be used to help steer and propel when the boat is being rowed.

"The Blue Boat" is a classic guide's boat in its finish. It is painted an unobtrusive color. At the end of the century increasing numbers of guideboats appeared on Adirondack waters in unlikely colors such as orange and white, or with varnish instead of paint. These boats were generally ordered by the sports themselves, who were taking to

"The Blue Boat," 1892

guiding themselves as the woods became more civilized, or to purchasing guideboats as pleasure craft. These rowers often had as much appreciation for the boat as an object of art as they did for its qualities as a good rowboat, and wanted to exhibit the extraordinary quality of craftsmanship that went into it.

On extended hunting or fishing excursions through the Adirondacks, scenes such as this one became familiar. The sports, such as the gentleman in the foreground, were expected to carry the duffel. The novices among them thought they were getting off easily; carrying, or backing, the boat seemed, as one put it, "as impossible as carrying a man-o'-war." What they didn't real-

"Raquette River. At Sweeney Carry," 1888, photograph by Seneca Ray Stoddard

ize was that while the boat weighed from fifty to seventy-five pounds it was "compact and in one bundle," and perfectly balanced. The sport's load was likely to consist of a gun or two, a packbasket or knapsack, a couple of fishing rods, and a portmanteau or coat—all of which invariably, halfway across the carry, began to go their separate ways.

At the shore the guide gently put the boat down with the stern and most of the bottom in the water, as the guide on the left in this photo is doing, loaded it with gear, and prepared for departure. The sport was instructed to step into the boat and walk down its centerline to the stern seat, keeping his weight low and holding on to each gunwale for balance. When he was safely in place, the guide, hands on gunwales near the bow, one knee on the bow deck, pushed off from shore with the other foot and gracefully vaulted into the boat. Seated in the bow seat, he took up the oars, turned the boat around, and started rowing.

A scene such as this must have become indelibly imprinted on the minds of hundreds of sportsmen and tourists of Homer's day, especially since the posture and method of the rower was so different from what they were used to seeing in other types of rowing craft. The guide in this photo, clearly identified by his badge, is sitting almost on the bottom of the boat, the soles of his outstretched feet almost touching the boot soles of the photographer-passenger. A guideboat has little freeboard and is initially tippy because of its narrow bottom; the occu-

"The Way It Looks From The Stern Seat," ca. 1890, photograph by Seneca Ray Stoddard

pants must sit low to preserve stability. The guide must cross his hands on the recovery of each stroke; the boat is narrow (for speed) and to be long enough for good leverage the inboard ends of the oars must be more than half the width of the boat. The city sport used to conventional rowboats also would have wondered at the way in which the oars are "pinned" to the outwales. They cannot be twisted in their sockets to cut wind resistance or pulled inboard to shorten them in a narrow passage. The first time his guide dropped the oars to help him land a speckled trout, however, he would have appreciated guideboat oarlocks as the oars trailed gently behind the boat instead of floating out of reach.

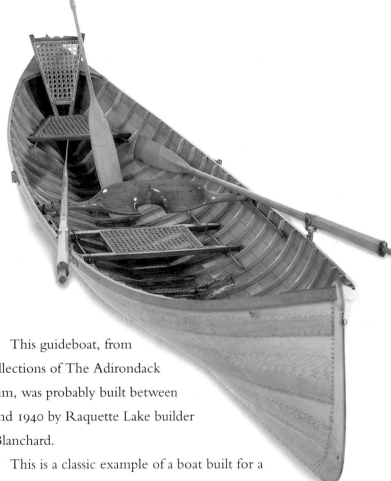

Adirondack guideboat

This guideboat, from the collections of The Adirondack Museum, was probably built between 1910 and 1940 by Raquette Lake builder John Blanchard.

This is a classic example of a boat built for a sportsman, rather than a guide. It is finished "bright," rather than with paint, and has the owner's monogram carved into the deck, paddle, and yoke. Long Laker George W. Smith, the builder, was one of the region's finest craftsmen. He built this boat around 1895 for a New York lawyer who summered on Blue Mountain Lake.

By the 1890s, when Homer painted "The Adirondack Guide,"
the independent woodsmen Murray had written about had become
the aristocrats of the profession and one had to reserve their time as
much as a year in advance. An Adirondack guide not only knew the
way through the woods, but saw to every aspect of his client's sporting, comfort, and safety. He could find trout and deer in abundance,
make comfortable camps where the sport could sleep on a bed of fra-
grant balsam boughs under a weatherproof roof of spruce bark, cook
potatoes and biscuits to go with the trout and venison, and provide
the transportation, both the vessel and the power.

There were many other guides in the woods, however, who
were much more accessible. House guides worked by the season for a
private camp or association, such as the North Woods Club, and were
often on call for caretaking chores in addition to guiding duties for
the owner or the guests. Somewhat below them in status were the
hotel guides, who worked out of the public hotels springing up
throughout the woods, and who took guests out from the hotel
dock—usually just for a day-long picnic excursion or a trip to the
next hotel.

The guide in this painting is probably a house guide for the
North Woods Club. He is not rowing an Adirondack guideboat, but
a humbler craft, a flat-bottomed, blunt-nosed punt. Homer depicted
these punts in several of his Adirondack paintings. They are basically
like boxes with upturned ends. The North Woods Club, like many

"The Adirondack Guide," 1894

other private preserves, probably had several of these sturdy craft at each pond so that members would always have a boat for fishing or hunting without the labor of "backing" one in.

The Adirondack guideboat is the best known of the North Woods craft painted by Homer, but not the only type. Unlike many artists who put in their pictures the boats they were familiar with or that they felt their audiences wanted to see (A. F. Tait, whose paintings were widely published by Currier and Ives, almost always featured the romantic birchbark canoe), Homer seems to have painted what he saw. The guideboat was ideally suited for swift, easy travel over long distances with substantial loads, but it was fragile, tippy, and expensive. Sturdier, heavier, cheaper boats were more practical at places like clubs or camps where a boat could be left on shore for fishing.

In "The Adirondack Guide" Homer painted a punt, and in "An Adirondack Lake" he painted a dugout canoe. Guideboat influence shows in both craft. The punt is being rowed with guideboat-style pinned oarlocks, and the dugout is propelled with a long-bladed guideboat-style paddle, seen here in the hands of the guide on the log. The dugout also has in it another standard piece of guideboat equipment, a jacklight. Constructed of a lantern on a pole, usually with some sort of reflector, the jacklight was mounted in the bow of the boat and used for night hunting of deer. The animal, mesmerized by the bright light, was an easy mark.

"An Adirondack Lake," 1870

The Fishing Was Superb

No one knows *what game there is in a trout, unless he has fought it out, matching such a rod against a three-pound fish, with forty feet of water underneath, and a clear, unimpeded sweep around him! Ah, then it is that one discovers what will and energy lie within the mottled skin of a trout, and what a miracle of velocity he is when roused.* —Adirondack Murray

Opposite: "Leaping Trout" (detail), 1889

Homer went to the North Woods Club not solely to paint but also, and perhaps primarily, to fish. He was an expert fly-fisherman. Some indication of his seriousness in sportfishing survives in the club register of June 1900. There, in a list of his catch, he drew a picture of the hook he had used to catch a 6¼-pound pike, specifying size and type.

For centuries the art of sport-fishing has been placed on a higher plane than most other individual sports, and fly-fishing in some views ranks highest of all. The primacy of fly-fishing rests on the understanding that it epitomizes the union of the active and the contemplative life. It is hardly matched among human endeavors as a means of taking the measure of one's intellectual and manual powers operating in alliance, with nothing of real import at risk. The intellectual aspect of sportfishing derives from the need to conceptualize accurately the behavior of fish and the conditions of fishing, taking account of stillness and motion, surface, and depth at the margin of land and water, while intent on capturing life in one world and

"Fish Hook," 1900

bringing it into another. The image of the thoughtful fisher has a
rich history in the arts, especially in books that Homer would have
known at first or second hand. Izaac Walton cast his essay of practical
philosophy, *The Compleat Angler*, in the form of a conversation about
fishing; John Bunyan used a metaphor of angling to justify his use of
allegory in *The Pilgrim's Progress;* and Henry Thoreau introduced a
self-absorbed fisher into the Concord River as he and his brother set
out on their week's journey.

Sportfishing, and above all fly-fishing, also requires exceptional skills of manual dexterity. The selection and tying of flies, the
timing, the casting, the hooking, the playing, the netting—all this

depends for success on the experienced, finely tuned interplay of eye, hand, and mind. So does painting in watercolors. Homer doubtless saw parallels between what he did as a watercolorist and what he did as a fly-fisher.

Homer's exceptional powers of observation coupled with an extraordinary command of the watercolor medium produced between 1889 and 1900 a group of paintings of fish and fishing that are among the wonders of American art. His "Leaping Trout," "Mink Pond," and "Casting, 'A Rise'" are representative. They have nothing to do with the by-then old subject of camp life, and everything to do with Homer's sensibilities as fisherman and painter. But while they capture with remarkable authenticity the behavior of fish and the experience of fly-fishing, as sportfishermen have attested for nearly a century, they also attract a far greater number of viewers who know or care little about fishing. Part of the appeal surely comes from Homer's bravura technique.

Durham Ranger

Silver Doctor

Consider the watercolor "Casting, 'A Rise'." Homer drew the serpentine line of the fisherman's cast by cutting through the washes of color with a point to reveal the white paper beneath. He did this in a single rapid gesture in which any miscalculation, hesitancy, or rush would have ruined the illusion that the line is cast toward the viewer. The multiple washes are complex in their sequence and manipulation. The composition is to a significant extent the result of cropping. Although the work had its origins in keen observation and

"Leaping Trout," 1889

"Casting, 'A Rise'," 1889

rapid execution, its completion required deliberate and close calcula-
tion. It is one of Homer's great achievements that he not only pre-
served the spontaneity of his original watercolor sketches as he
"finished" them in his studio at Prout's Neck, usually some weeks
after his original work, but actually heightened their sense of imme-
diacy. Having brushed, soaked, blotted, scraped, touched, and
trimmed, he seems to have taken pride in these watercolors as hand-
crafted objects. The tenor of the times would have encouraged this.

In the summer of 1893, Homer and his brother Charles traveled to Quebec rather than to the Adirondacks and began a decade in
which the artist for the most part alternated summer visits to Minerva
one year with excursions to prime fishing country in Canada the
next. In 1893 they went to the Tourilli Fish and Game Club in dense
forest beyond the village of Saint Raymond, some thirty miles west of
Quebec City. The North Woods Club was accessible by road and

THE PLACE SUITS ME *as if it was made for me by a kind of providence.* —WINSLOW HOMER

"Grand Discharge, Lake St. John, Province of Quebec," ca. 1902

"Canoe in Rapids," 1897

THIS IS NOT A LITTLE POCKET *of wilderness like the Adirondacks, but something vast and primitive. You do not cross it, from one railroad to another, by a line of hotels. You go in by one river as far as you like, or dare; and then you turn and come back again by another river, making haste to get out before your provisions are exhausted. The lake itself is the cradle of the mighty Saguenay, an inland sea, thirty miles across and nearly round, lying in the broad limestone basin north of the Laurentian Mountains.* —HENRY VAN DYKE

wagons, but the Tourilli Club, in more rugged terrain, required a long trek on foot accompanied by guides. In the Adirondacks, Homer had enjoyed the company of women, children, and babes in arms, but now, at Lake Tourilli, he became part of an exclusive men's sporting club deep in a wilderness. The fishing was superb. The brothers built a cabin there, and returned in 1895, 1897, and 1902. In those years they also went farther into Quebec, to Lake St. John, the source of the grand Saguenay River, more than a hundred miles north of Quebec City. At Lake Tourilli, Homer kept a purpose-built flat-bottomed boat, a kind of punt, and painted and fished from it. At Lake St. John and on the Saguenay, he traveled by canoe, paddled by guides.

Tomah Jo

That Homer first went to Canada to fish and not to paint explains the absence of any Canadian works from 1893. But his succeeding visits brought forth a rich variety of watercolors, all distinct in feeling and subject from those he painted in the Adirondacks. Many of them depicted fishing, or travel by canoe with fishing gear. In "A Good Pool, Saguenay River," he returns to the idea of a leaping fish as the dominant element of a painting, but now it is a ouananiche salmon rather than a trout, and now he shows the fisherman who plays him, leaning in rhythm with his silvery combatant as his guides steady the canoe in the Saguenay's violent waters. If Homer had ever fished such a powerfully moving river before, he had never painted it, but now, as in his "Grand Discharge," in which his subject is set at one of the two dramatic outpourings of Lake St. John that feed the Saguenay, he painted the rush and foam and driving energy with a knowledge informed at least a little by the experience of painting the sea pounding the shore below his studio in Maine.

Homer's "Trout Fishing, Lake St. John" is a variant of his Adirondack "Casting, 'A Rise'," changed in nearly every respect to convey a subtlely different sense of place, activity, and mood. As in many of his Quebec watercolors of 1895, he reduced his palette to a monochromatic, but richly expressive range of silvery grays, tones that capture northern light and seem right for the density of the forest and the vastness of the land. The still mirror-like surface of the lake will soon be broken by a splash and the fisherman's contest with a determined trout.

"Trout Fishing, Lake St. John, Quebec," 1895

"A Good Pool, Saguenay River," 1895

"The Guide," 1889

Homer's watercolor box

On 23 June 1910, in failing health, Winslow Homer arrived in the Adirondacks for the last time. He had traveled by rail from Prout's Neck, Maine, to North Creek, New York, then by wagon nearly nineteen miles over rough roads to the village of Minerva and into the forest beyond. He had come to fish and to restore his health, not to draw or paint. Less than three months later he would be dead.

Winslow Homer had transformed a minor American subject of the 1850s—Adirondack camp life—into the most mature and brilliantly expressed portrayal of man at home in the forest that we know. He had come to the subject in good part through his interest in fishing, and it was fishing that led him on to the Adirondacks and Quebec, where he succeeded more than any other artist of his time or since in distilling into pictures the excitement that wilderness—nature at its freest—arouses in Americans. And he did this in a sequence of works, nearly all in watercolor, that from their first showings to the present have seemed so truthful, so eloquent, and so moving in what they say, and how they say it, that they have no peers.

Index of Illustrations

THE ADIRONDACK MUSEUM, a regional museum of history and art, is open daily Memorial Day weekend until mid-October from 9:30 A.M. until 5:30 P.M. Researchers are welcome by appointment year-round, Monday-Friday, 9:00-5:00. For more information contact: The Adirondack Museum, Blue Mountain Lake, NY 12812. Telephone: (518) 352-7311.

The Adirondack Museum boat collection has been called the finest assemblage of non-powered inland pleasure craft in the country. The 197 boats include 58 guideboats and 59 canoes and all represent boating in the Adirondack region.

THE AMERICAN MUSEUM OF FLY FISHING, a museum dedicated to preserving the rich heritage of fly-fishing, is open daily from the last Saturday in April until the last day of October from 10:00 A.M. until 4:00 P.M. During the rest of the year, the Museum is open Monday-Friday, 10:00-4:00. researchers are welcome by appointment year-round. For more information contact: The American Museum of Fly Fishing, Manchester, VT 05254. Telephone: (802) 362-3300.

The Museum serves as a repository for, and conservator to, the world's largest collection of angling and angling-related objects. Rods, reels, and flies, as well as tackle, art, books, manuscripts, and photographs form the major components of the Museum's collections.

DAVID TATHAM is Professor of Fine Arts at Syracuse University. He is the author of many studies of American painting and graphic art of the nineteenth century including *Winslow Homer and the Illustrated Book* (Syracuse University Press, 1992) and the forthcoming *Winslow Homer in the Adirondacks*.

HALLIE E. BOND is Curator of Collections and Boats at the Adirondack Museum. In charge of the boat collection since 1987, she curated the major permanent exhibit "Boats and Boating in the Adirondacks," which opened in 1991, and wrote the book of the same name, published in 1995. She lives at the head of Long Lake with her son and husband, and goes out in a canoe, Good-Boat, or guideboat whenever the lake is clear of ice.

TOM ROSENBAUER has been a fly-fisher all his life. His books include *The Orvis Fly-Fishing Guide, Reading Trout Streams, Prospecting for Trout*, and *Casting Illusions*. He has been published in *Field & Stream, Fly Fisherman, Fly Rod & Reel, Audubon*, and many other magazines. He is vice-president of merchandising for the Orvis Company and a trustee of The American Museum of Fly Fishing.

RECOMMENDED READING:

The Adirondack Reader, copyright © 1982 by Paul Jamieson. The Adirondack Mountain Club, Inc., Lake George, New York

Adventures in the Wilderness, William H. H. Murray, edited by William K. Verner. Copyright © 1989 by Syracuse University Press